Main Character Energy

Temi Wilkey

I0141074

methuen | drama

LONDON • NEW YORK • OXFORD • NEW DELHI • SYDNEY

METHUEN DRAMA

Bloomsbury Publishing Plc, 50 Bedford Square, London, WC1B 3DP, UK
Bloomsbury Publishing Inc, 1359 Broadway, New York, NY 10018, USA
Bloomsbury Publishing Ireland, 29 Earlsfort Terrace, Dublin 2,
D02 AY28, Ireland

BLOOMSBURY, METHUEN DRAMA and the Methuen
Drama logo are trademarks of Bloomsbury Publishing Plc.

First published by Methuen Drama 2025

Cover design by Michael Julings

Cover Photography by Jade Ang Jackman

No rights in incidental music or songs contained in the work are hereby
granted and performance rights for any performance/presentation
whatsoever must be obtained from the respective copyright owners.

All rights whatsoever in this play are strictly reserved and application
for performance etc. should be made before rehearsals to Curtis Brown
Group Ltd, Haymarket House, 28–29 Haymarket, London, SW1Y 4SP.
No performance may be given unless a licence has been obtained

A catalogue record for this book is available from the British Library.

A catalog record for this book is available from the Library of Congress.

ISBN: PB: 978-1-3506-1419-2
ePDF: 978-1-3506-1421-5
eBook: 978-1-3506-1420-8

Series: Modern Plays

Typeset by Mark Heslington Ltd, Scarborough, North Yorkshire

For product safety related questions contact
productsafety@bloomsbury.com.

To find out more about our authors and books visit
www.bloomsbury.com and sign up for our newsletters.

Main Character Energy was first performed at the Edinburgh Festival Fringe on 1 August 2024 at Paines Plough's Roundabout at Summerhall. The show was previewed at the Yard Theatre, London on 4 July 2024 and then the Belgrade Theatre, Coventry on 18 July 2024 with the following team:

Writer & Performer	Temi Wilkey
Director & Dramaturg	Ragevan Vasan
Movement Director	Bambi Phillips
Set & Costume Designer	Jasmine Araujo
Lighting Designer	Lauren Faux
Sound Designer	Xana
Stage Manager	Roshan Conn
Dramatherapist	Wabriya King
Producer	Bobby Harding

The show was restaged at Soho Theatre, London on 25 February 2025 with the following team:

Writer & Performer	Temi Wilkey
Director & Dramaturg	Ragevan Vasan
Movement Director	Bambi Phillips
Set Designer	Jasmine Araujo
Costume Designer	Annika Thiems
Lighting Designer	Lauren Faux
Sound Designer	Xana
Stage Manager	Roshan Conn
Movement Support	Amani Cosmo
Assistant Producer	Kam Miller
Producer	Bobby Harding

Supported using public funding by Arts Council England, with thanks to the following people:

Michael Julings, Jade Ang Jackman, Mia Maxwell, Tell Tale Beauty, Sharon McHendry PR, Bread and Butter PR, Stephanie Sian Smith, Ciáran C, Tommy Ga-Ken Wan, the team at DMLK, Rachel Rebecca Jones.

Shout out to the Royal Court and Hawkwood Centre for Future Thinking for helping us host our Taking Up Space residency, Chisenhale Dance Space for rehearsal space, Soho Theatre for the early sharing space, the Yard and the Belgrade Theatres for hosting our previews and, of course, Paines Plough for their unwavering support and guidance.

Temi Wilkey – Writer & Performer

Temi Wilkey is an award-winning playwright, actress and comedienne. She studied English at Cambridge before training with the National Youth Theatre REP company in 2014.

Temi was a member of the Royal Court's Young Writers' Group in 2017 and wrote her debut play, *The High Table*, at the course's culmination. It was produced at the Bush Theatre in Lynette Linton's debut season, and won Temi The Stage Debut Award for Best Writer in 2020.

She also co-founded and co-directed the Drag King company Pecs, performing in the sell-out runs of their shows at venues including Soho Theatre, The Yard and Tate Britain before leaving the company in 2019.

Temi wrote an episode of Netflix's *Sex Education* S3 for which she was nominated for an NAACP Image Award for Outstanding Writing in a Comedy Series. She also wrote two episodes for Disney Plus's *Wedding Season*. In 2021 she was on the BFI Flare x BAFTA Crew programme mentored by Russell T. Davies and was named one of the Forbes 30 Under 30.

Ragevan Vasan – Director & Dramaturg

Ragevan Vasan is a British Tamil actor and director from South London.

He is a triple Off West End Theatre Award nominated actor. Theatre acting credits include *The Animal Kingdom* and *Little Scratch* (Hampstead Theatre), *Name, Place, Animal, Thing* (Almeida Theatre), *Living Newspaper* (Royal Court Theatre), *I Wanna Be Yours* (Bush Theatre), *Love for Love* (RSC), *Hurling Rubble at the Sun, Hurling Rubble at the Moon* (Park Theatre). His screen acting credits include Tim Burton's *Dumbo*, Emmy-nominated *Andor* and BAFTA-winning *Save Me*.

As director, his credits include projects for Theatre Deli, 5x5 and Ricochet Theatre Company. This is his debut full-length production.

Bambi Phillips – Movement Director

Bambi Jordan Phillips is a producer, movement artist, model and DJ interested in driving artistic work for social change. Bambi is a cornerstone of the London Ballroom Scene, an advocate, mentor and authority for the community, where she is Mother of the Kiki House of Laveaux. From organising at a grassroots level to internationally acclaimed venues, Bambi believes in voguing as a direct connection to embodied trans-ancestry. She creates work that explores identity and the deconstruction of learned ideas of gender, sexuality, desire and race. She is often found pumping between live performance, sound and moving image.

Credits include: As movement director, theatre: *As You Like It* (The Globe), *Sundown Kiki* and *Sundown KiKi Reloaded* (Young Vic), *Sound of the Underground* (Royal Court Theatre). As choreographer, theatre: *Marie Laveaux* (Stanley Arts), *like the water* (Raze Collective commission), *Me and MJ* (Giddy Up commission). As choreographer and performer, film: *By Earth Sea and Air*, *The heart wants what the heart wants* (Adham Faramawy), *Life Cycles of Rainbows* (India Sky).

As producer: *The Black Obsidian Ball* at Rivoli Ballroom (part of We Are Lewisham, presented by Lewisham Council and the Albany as part of the Mayor's London Borough of Culture 2022), *The C'est Chic Kiki Ball* (part of Nile Rodgers Meltdown Festival, Southbank Centre) and *On the Block KiKi Ball* (part of Peckham Festival).

Jasmine Araujo – Set Designer

Jasmine Araujo is a London-based performance designer working across theatre, dance, installation, film and TV. She was awarded the Max Rayne Design Bursary at the National

Theatre, where she was Associate Designer on *The LeftBehinds* and worked on productions including *Hamlet*. Her design credits include *Kabel* (Sadler's Wells), *Lady Dealer* (Bush Theatre), *Rapunzel* (Theatre Peckham), *The Shoemaker* (Welsh National Opera) and *An End to a Beginning* (The Walk with Amal). Prop design credits include *Beneatha's Place* (Young Vic).

Annika Thiems – Costume Designer

Annika Thiems is a London-based textile artist whose surrealist costumes and sculptures delve into the absurd and unconscious, often tipping into the camp and delirious. Drawing on theatrical devices and psychoanalytic theory, she creates uncanny personas that act as projection screens for illusions and desires. Her work has been shown at the Victoria & Albert Museum, Tate Britain, No. 9 Cork Street and Sadler's Wells, and featured in *The World of Interiors*, *The New York Times*, the *Guardian* and *Interview* magazine. She collaborates with visual artists and performers, including Damsel Elysium, Himali Singh Soin & David Soin Tappeser, and Elisabeth Mulenga, to develop characters and narratives through custom garments and tapestries. Raised in East Frisia, Germany, as the fourth generation in a family of upholsterers, Thiems began sewing early – an influence that shapes her experimental approach to tailoring and soft construction.

She holds degrees in Psychology and Curating and received the 2019 NEON Curatorial Award.

Lauren Faux – Lighting Designer

Lauren Faux is a Stockport-born lighting designer and technician based in London. She trained in Lighting Design at the Royal Central School of Speech and Drama, graduating in 2018. Her design credits include *The Second Woman* (Young Vic), *Burgerz* (UK and international tour),

Blubber (Roundhouse, WIP), *The Sun Does Shine* (Hackney Empire) and *Fatty Fat Fat* (UK tour).

Xana – Sound Designer

Theatre credits: *After Sunday* (Belgrade Theatre); *Alterations* (National Theatre); *Not Your Superwoman*, *Speed*, *The Real Ones*, *My Father's Fable*, *Elephant*, *Sleepova*, *The P Word*, *Strange Fruit* (Bush Theatre); *The Architect* (ATC/GDIF); *Pig Heart Boy* (Unicorn Theatre); *Shifters*, *Barcelona* (Duke of York's Theatre); *Beautiful Thing* (Theatre Royal Stratford East); *Imposter 22*, *Word:Play*, *Living Newspaper #4* (Royal Court); *Intimate Apparel*, *The Trials*, *Marys Seacole* (Donmar Warehouse); *Anna Karenina* (Edinburgh Lyceum/Bristol Old Vic); *Sundown Kiki*, *Earthworks*, *Sundown Kiki Reloaded*, *The Collaboration*, *Changing Destiny*, *Fairview*, *Ivan and the Dogs* (Young Vic); *Burgerz* (Hackney Showroom); *King Troll [The Fawn]*, *Everyday* (Deafinitely) (New Diorama Theatre); *Blood Knot*, *Guards at the Taj* (Orange Tree Theatre); *Samuel Takes a Break* (Yard Theatre).

Awards include: BBTA winner for Best Sound Design 2023 and 2024; BBTA nomination for Best Musical Direction for *Alterations*, Offie Award winner for *King Troll*, *Shifters* and *Guards at the Taj*; Offie Award nominations for *Sleepova*, *The P Word* and *Blood Knot*; Olivier Award for Best New Production in Affiliate Theatre for *The P Word* and *Sleepova*.

Wabriya King – Dramatherapist

Wabriya King is a qualified dramatherapist (Roehampton University), actress (Oxford School of Drama), creative facilitator and Reiki practitioner, who combines her experience to support creatives alongside the rehearsal and performance period.

Wabriya is the Associate Dramatherapist for the Bush Theatre and has supported all productions since 2021.

Dramatherapy support credits include:

Theatre: *Born with Teeth* (Wyndham Theatre); *Intimate Apparel, Love and Other Acts of Violence, The Trials, Clyde's* (Donmar Warehouse); *Alterations, Blues for an Alabama Sky* (National Theatre); *Elektra, Barcelona, Romeo & Juliet* (Duke of York's Theatre); *Slave Play* (Noël Coward Theatre); *Shifters* (Duke of York's Theatre/Bush Theatre); *A Strange Loop* (Barbican Centre); *Otherland, Roots, Look Back in Anger, Portia Coughlan, King Lear, Alma Mater, Romeo and Juliet, The Secret Life of Bees* (Almeida Theatre); *Red Pitch* (@sohoplace/Bush Theatre); *For Black Boys Who Have Considered Suicide When the Hue Gets Too Heavy* (Garrick Theatre, Royal Court, New Diorama Theatre); *School Girls; Or, The African Mean Girls Play* (Lyric Hammersmith); *Wicked, Cabaret, Hamilton, Moulin Rouge, MJ the Musical* (West End); *Just for One Day* (Old Vic); *Now, I See, Beautiful Thing, Tambo & Bones* (Theatre Royal Stratford East); *Falkland Sound, The Empress, Julius Caesar* (RSC); *Cowbois* (Royal Court/RSC); *Samskara, Samuel Takes a Break, The Flea* (The Yard); *Bootycandy* (Gate Theatre); *Drive Your Plow Over the Bones of the Dead* (Complicité); *Blue* (ENO); *Further than the Furthest Thing* (Young Vic); *Fantastically Great Women Who Changed the World* (The Other Palace/UK tour); *Becoming Nancy* (Birmingham Rep); *Revealed* (Belgrade Theatre); *SHED: Exploded View* (Manchester Royal Exchange); *Matthew Bourne's Romeo + Juliet* (New Adventures); *Family Tree* (Actors Touring Company).

Film: *The Changing Room* (Anima Goli Productions), *Empire of Light* (Searchlight Pictures) and *Chevalier* (Element Pictures).

Bobby Harding – Producer

Bobby Harding is a Walsall-born, trans non-binary producer working across theatre and live performance. They produce bold, community-driven work centring under-represented voices and platforming ground-shattering artists. To date, they have raised nearly £400k for artists and theatre companies across the UK.

Recent projects include *Main Character Energy* by Temi Wilkey (Roundabout @ Summerhall, Soho Theatre, Bristol Old Vic, Chichester Festival Theatre, Sheffield Theatres), *Luv Shannon X* by Joseph Wilson (Seventeen Gallery), *The Belt of Venus* by Kenya Sterling and Joseph Wilson (Newington Green Meeting House) and *Metamorphoses* by JimmyJ (The Cockpit).

As an associate producer their credits include *Double Drop* by Lisa Jên Brown (Summerhall, Edinburgh Festival Fringe), *Blueprints* by Ashlee Elizabeth-Lolo (Pleasance Courtyard and Pleasance London) and *Vermin* by Benny Ainsworth (Arcola Theatre).

Bobby is also the Fundraising and Grants Lead for London Trans+ Pride and was selected to be part of Stage One's Bridge the Gap 2025/26 cohort.

Main Character Energy

Notes on the Text

Play texts are funny things. They attempt to capture a live theatrical experience that is, by nature, ephemeral.

I didn't write this show in verse. But, as I edit the play text, I've come to realise that I performed it in verse.

Some of my favourite comedic performers have recently led me to believe that comedy is all about poetry – the precision and rhythm of a stand-up's language are a big part of what makes a joke land.

I do not profess to be a stand-up. But this show is (almost) all about its humour.

So, despite not having written the show in verse, in an attempt to capture the comedic rhythm of its performance, I have rendered a lot of the play text into it.

Verse heightens, it elevates. It makes everything romantic. Which feels, dare I say, *indulgent.*

If this show is ever performed again by anyone besides me, the performer must feel free to bring their own comedic cadence to it. But here's the sheet music, as a reference.

[Square brackets denote where something can be changed for future productions.]

Notes on the 'Play'

I think of this show as a 'play'. It is full of play. It is not that serious. Except for when it is.

It is satire, a loving parody of the one-woman show. In short, have fun with it!

Though it is steeped in irony, it must all be played in earnest. It's a tightrope walk but it is really fun to *walk*.

Say it with chest but also with jest.

Notes on Character(s)

Temi is a heightened, more camp and indulgent version of the playwright herself.

If this show is ever to be produced without Temi Wilkey as the performer, the name of the character must be changed to the first name of the performer. This performer must play a heightened, more camp and indulgent version of themselves.

To play this part, the performer must be black, physical, playful and have an intimate relationship to camp.

They can be any gender but they truly can *not* be straight. Soz x.

With the writer's permission, details of the story can be changed to suit a fabulated, fictionalised autobiography of the performer's life to suit the conceit of the text.

Stage Manager is a role taken on by the show's real stage manager. They have very few but very important lines. They are matter of fact, gentle but firm.

Be very kind to them for taking this on.

From a symbolic standpoint, the Stage Manager's relationship with Temi works best if the Stage Manager is white or white-passing.

Notes on the Relationship with the Audience

There is no fourth wall. The performer looks at the audience, loves to see them seeing her. This show is at its best when it feels *live*.

We are all very present and in the room. Ad-libs and improvisations are not only welcome but necessary.

Notes on the Set

This show was originally performed in the round. This should be done where possible but, if not, a cheeky thrust will do. The audience on several (ideally all) sides should feel, at times, incredible for the performer and, at times, over-exposing.

The set should be minimal but give the impression of a plush boudoir. The lighting design should be dynamic and elevate this minimalism.

Notes on Costume

It must be comfy but fabulous.

Preface

As a black woman, I believe that it is radical to be self-indulgent.

I made *Main Character Energy* in a year when I dared myself to be audacious. Writing a self-proclaimedly self-indulgent one-woman show, for myself to perform in, forced me to step into my power, taught me so much – it exploded my artistic world.

This is truly just the beginning.

Main Character Energy and its forthcoming sequels are all about love.

This one is about self-love.

This show is for the black girls, the brown-skinned girls, the dark-skinned girls, the trans girls and the trans femmes.

For the girls with music in them.
That people pretend they can't hear.

It's for the little black girl in Dublin who was overlooked by the official when everyone else received their gymnastics medals.

It's for Fran.

It's for you.

It's for anyone who has ever wanted to feel seen, glamorous or celebrated.

But this show, when it started off, was for me.
This show is *so* me.
This show is full of myself.

And I am so grateful I got to make it.

An empty stage, preferably in the round, with a pink ottoman, a fluffy rug and a gorgeous satin blanket cascading from the chest. All of this is off-centre.

The pre-state music is boomy, bassy and affirming. Bad bitch tunes, blacketty black. As the house lights dim, the sound of **Temi***'s own voice comes in over a god mic.*

Temi (*over the god mic*)   Ladies and gentlemen, distinguished guests. Please welcome to the stage the beautiful, the talented, the criminally undercast . . . Temi Wilkey.

Temi *enters and self-indulgently promenades around the space in a fabulous costume, underscored by Nicki Minaj's 'Moment 4 Life'.*

The audience cheers her on. She seems to look each of them in the eye. She gratefully takes in this moment. Her moment. At times she lip-syncs to some of the lyrics.

She removes a layer of her glamorous regalia, hangs it up ceremoniously and then takes centre stage.

She strikes a pose.

Temi   ACT ONE: My journey to the stage.

Blackout.

This first act must be played with the clunky precision and utter conviction of a devised GCSE drama performance.

An abstract soundscape montage of **Temi***'s life which ends in the heartbeat of her embryo.*

We are about to begin at the beginning: 'The birth of **Temi***.'*

Lights up.

An instrumental of Victoria Monét's 'Moment' underscores . . .

Temi   July 1992 –

I was born on a Monday.
Monday's Child.
Some say that makes me 'fair of face'.
Others would disagree . . .
But we'll get to that later.

I was *born* for the stage.

Are stars born?
Gaynor, Streisand, Gaga.
Or are they *made*?
When I was eight years old,
I got a hernia.

The underscore abruptly cuts –

Do you know what a hernia is?

It's a painful lump
That can develop
In your lower abdomen.

They're more common amongst
Middle-aged men
Than eight-year-old children.

And they generally develop
When you've been doing a lot of
Heavy lifting.

On the day I was diagnosed
My mother was puzzled.
To her, it was a mystery.
But I knew.
Heavy lifting?

I got a hernia because I was
Carrying all the kids in our rehearsals
For the school play.

Every day after school
These kids would come in late,
No charisma,
None of them had learnt their lines!

'This isn't reception anymore, Millie!
You can't get by by
Futtering your eyelashes
Like you did for the Nativity.
You're a talentless ham
And an embarrassment to the school!'

I tried to tell my mother this,
That the reason I had a hernia
Was because of
Dumb bitches like Milli.

But she was too busy booking in
The appointment for my surgery.
SURGERY? I'm eight years old.
They're going to cut me open.
I'm going to DIE.

But what ensued
Was a fate
Worse than death.
The day of the appointment
Was the same day . . .
As the school play.

I *begged*. On my knees, I begged.
This was my big break.
I was playing Peaseblossom
In *A Midsummer Night's Dream*.

(I would have liked
To have been one of the lovers.
But it was still early.
This was year four.
If I killed, like I knew I would,

I was on track to getting a lead part
In the Year 6 leavers play.)

I couldn't miss this performance.
I couldn't.
But there was no other date available.
And I was in *visible* pain.

As I limped to the car
I tried to pretend
I was fine. Hernia Schmernia!
But my mother wouldn't listen.
She never listened.

The only theatre I went to on that
Late spring evening was
. . . The operating theatre.

As they put me under
And I gasped down
The general anaesthetic
The bright, surgical lights felt
Almost . . . Like a spotlight.

She mimes falling asleep. She wakes up.

When I came to. The first thing I did was look at the time.
5 p.m. We were early. We could make it!

Eight years old and *doped* out of my mind –
I clambered out of my hospital bed.
Ripped the IV drip from my veins.

All so I could run to the stage.

In the car I screamed at my mother to – (*as if she is heavily drugged*) 'Drive me to school, Mummy, I can do it. I can do it.'

But she refused.
I cried all the way home.
And I never forgave her.

There is a lighting and sound transition that transports the audience to a space more akin to cabaret. Jazzy piano music comes in to underscore that reflects this shift.

This is often the point in the show where **Temi** *ushers in late comers. After, sincerely, welcoming them in as she grabs a microphone.*

Temi   Good evening, everyone!

Welcome to my ground-breaking one-woman show *Main Character Energy.*

This is the story of my life.
How I came to be stood
Resplendent before you today.
It showcases my talents, my emotional range
And my Curriculum Vitae.
So that I can finally get the kind of acting parts
I deserve.

How are you liking it so far?

[*This is a moment where* **Temi** *grounds the audience in the space, the fact that the show is truly live. It should feel like everything she's saying is off the cuff. Change the name of the venue or theatre shape at your will. But here's what the text was for Soho Theatre.*]

It is so good to be here at Soho Theatre. In the round! It's more like an oval really. It's an eye. Eye of the storm. Eye of the tiger. All eyes on me.

God, you are such a hot audience. I've done this show [*insert how many times before here*] and never, ever has there *ever* been such a good-looking crowd in. What the hell?

How dare you? I actually don't know how I'm going to get through the show. This is so distracting.

Stop! Stop looking at me! Ah! I'm shy.

*

I just got an idea.

Han? [*Insert the name of the* **Stage Manager** *– for now, let's call them Han.*] This is my lovely stage manager Han. Han, can you . . . cut the music for me please?

Stage Manager *cuts the music and the house lights may also be raised a touch.*

Temi   I loved hearing you clapping and cheering for me when I entered . . . But what I actually think will give me the energy I need for the rest of the show is something else. Will you do one thing for me?

She waits for the audience's genuine response. She playfully comments or ad-libs around it. Then –

Say my name.

After three, I want you all to whisper my name. Just my first name. Temi. Altogether, after three. OK?

Assuming the audience agrees, **Temi** *giddily stations herself centre stage and closes her eyes.*

One, two, three . . . Temi.

The audience collectively whispers **Temi**'s *name, in unison, and* **Temi** *becomes immediately possessed by the spirit of self-indulgence.*

Wow. That was magical.
It feels like you conjured my spirit
Out of my body
And my essence is all over us.
It's like I'm looking at an audience of mes.
I didn't think this audience could get any hotter
But it just did!

This show would be so different
If I was performing for an audience of mes.

Honestly, I think I would just masturbate.
For the full hour
Yeah.
And I think the audience of mes would just like

Cheer me on.
Just SCREAM my name over and over
As I came over and over and over again.

As an artist, at my core,
This is what I want to do.
When you make work
You have to please yourself first.
This feels artistically true.

This is what I want to do.
So maybe I've just got to do it . . .
What do you think?

She ad-libs to the genuine response of the audience:

If they cheer she gears herself up to pleasure herself for them, until this next thought occurs to her.

If there are any dissenting voices the thought occurs to her immediately.

But I don't think I can!
Like ethically. And . . . legally.
It pains me to say this and I hate to shatter
The beautiful illusion . . .
But you are not an audience of mes.
Some of you might not want to watch me masturbate.

I could say give me a cheer if you wanna see me come!

If the audience cheer **Temi** *looks really pleased.*

Temi   That is SO funny that you cheered!
I meant IF, *hypothetically,*
IF I were to say 'give me a cheer
If you wanna see me come!'

Even if every one of you
Was screaming for it
At the top of their lungs!
Some of you might be cheering for it
Because you feel pressured to.

By me.
You know, I have too much power in the situation.
As the person with the microphone.
Hello!

Even if I went up to each
And every one of you
Individually.

She approaches and eyeballs several audience members.

And I asked you
If you wanted to see me
Fuck myself for you
For art.

That would take too long.

And also, it's the same problem.
You know, the overwhelming hunger for it in the room.
And I can feel it.
Honestly, it is so hard not to oblige.
But that overwhelming hunger puts *pressure*
On each and every individual to say yes,
Even if they don't want it,
And that is not right.
That is not how consent works.
Unfortunately.

So . . . Yep. That's where feminism gets you.
CENSORSHIP.

Before the 'Me Too' movement.
I could have done this.
I could have masturbated for you all.
And, don't get me wrong,
I am so grateful for the movement.
Like yeah . . . 'me too'.

But what about . . . me? You know?
What about my art?
When are we going to have that conversation?

So yeah due to the *downsides* of feminism . . .
I'm just going to have to do what I prepared.

Which is *good*!

This show, as you've already seen, is great.
It's confessional,
Deeply personal.
It goes there.
It's meaningful.
But also edgy.
Cutting edge.
Cunty.
Cunt-emporary theatre.

Of the moment. But also *timeless*.
And at its beating heart is a flawed,
Unlikeable but somehow
Lovable character.
Me.

On with the show

Blackout.

Lights up as **Temi** *repeatedly whispers 'pas de bourrée, pas de bourrée' as she practises the dance step itself.*

Temi   Mummy, Mummy, look!

She does a brief stage-y dance.

She assumes the pose of her mother, typing on her laptop.

Temi (*as her mother*)   'Can't you see I'm working?'

Temi, *as her child self, looks disappointed. But, nevertheless persists.*

Temi   Daddy, Daddy, look!

She does a brief stage-y dance.

She assumes the 'out the door with a briefcase' pose of her father.

Temi (*as her father*)   'I've got to go.
I'm on call.
I've got to head into the hospital.
I'm a doctor.
REMEMBER?'

Temi *assumes the pose of her mother.*

Temi (*as her mother*)   'Me too. I too am a doctor,
I am a paediatrician
'That's a doctor for CHILDREN.
OTHER children.
All other children are more important than youuu.'

Temi (*as her father*)   Than yooou.

Temi (*as her mother*)   Than yooooouuuu.

Temi (*as herself*)   That's what they said.
Verbatim.
They were pragmatic parents,
They had no interest in my art.
A high mark on a maths test
Meant they would
Look up from their desk.
Give me a sweet minute of attention.

But I had to earn it.

The lights change and **Temi** *sings 'Taina', the theme song from the show.*

Temi

   I know I can't wait to
   see my name in lights
   No one's gonna stop me you'll see
   I will go far (what's your name?)
   Taina
   Taina
   I always had dreams of me being a star

   You'll be sayin' my name

See my star shining bright
I can reach any height
What's my name?'

The instrumental to 'Taina' continues to underscore **Temi***'s speech.*

Temi   Nickelodeon 2001.
Taina Morales was attending
The Manhattan School for Performing Arts
I was in the suburbs of London
Begging my parents to send me to the Brit School.
No surprises where that got me.

After school every day I'd tune into
All the black sitcoms on Trouble . . .
I'm talking *My Wife & Kids*, *One on One*, *The Parkers*,
Girlfriends, Sister, Sister.

Black child stars were setting my TV screen ablaze.
I was green with envy.

'Mom! Why couldn't you have emigrated to AMERICA!
You guys could have been doctors there!'

I could have been in Hollywood
Making my name.

I would have my own show,
Countless teen choice awards
And a severe eating disorder.

It was all I ever dreamt of.
Instead my mother had enrolled me
Into a Stagecoach . . .
Not because she saw my dramatic potential
But because one of my teachers had told her.

'Temi doesn't seem to have any friends.'

This was not true.
I had loads of friends.
My make-up artist,

My publicist,
My stylist.

I tried to tell my mother this
But she was aghast.
Turns out she thought that imaginary friends were
Troubling and
A bit pagan.

So she sent me to Stagecoach.
She thought sending me
To a Saturday school filled
With musical theatre kids
Would make me *less* weird.

The instrumental to 'Defying Gravity' plays and **Temi** *runs
around the stage in giddy glee before landing centre stage to sing
the triumphant final broomstick section, abruptly cutting at
'everyone deserves the chance –'.*

Flamboyant!
It made me *flamboyant.*
My mother's biggest regret was sending me to that
Stagecoach Barnet.
She never dreamt
I'd become this.

Classical piano music begins to play.

Years later
When I was training with the
Royal Youth Theatre
– Secondary school had been and gone.
I'd got a degree,
On my parents' insistence.

And now I was finally on the brink of becoming a
Professional actress.

The classical piano music fades down.

Our director told us:

'Opera singers have a repertoire.
They have parts on deck
That they train in but haven't played yet
So that when the time comes they are ready.

You should do the same.'

I took his heed.

She dramatically sets herself up onstage, looking bemused.

She then lip-syncs to various BBC clips of white women performing Shakespeare.

> I left no ring with her: what means this lady?
> Fortune forbid my outside have not charm'd her!
> She made good view of me; indeed, so much,
> That sure methought her eyes had lost her tongue,
> For she did speak in starts distractedly.
> She loves me, sure; the cunning of her passion
> Invites me in this churlish messenger.

She moves to a different position onstage, looking suitably mad.

> I am not mad: this hair I tear is mine;
> My name is Constance; I was Geffrey's wife;
> Young Arthur is my son, and he is lost.

She moves to a different position onstage, looking utterly infatuated.

> Thou knowest the mask of night is on my face,
> Else would a maiden blush bepaint my cheek
> For that which thou hast heard me speak tonight.
> Fain would I dwell on form, fain, fain deny . . .

The lip-sync track fades down and **Temi** *transitions from lip-syncing to speaking.*

It should, at first, feel almost as camp as the lip-sync and then slowly it should become grounded and deeply real. More real than the performer has felt onstage thus far.

What I have spoke; but farewell, compliment.
Dost thou love me? I know thou wilt say 'Ay',
And I will take thy word; yet, if thou swear'st,
Thou mayst prove false. At lovers' perjuries,
They say, Jove laughs. O gentle Romeo,
If thou dost love, pronounce it faithfully,
Or if thou think'st I am too quickly won,
I'll frown and be perverse and say thee nay,
So thou wilt woo, but else not for the world.
In truth, fair Montague, I am too fond,
And therefore thou mayst think my haviour light.
But trust me, gentleman, I'll prove more true
Than those that have more cunning to be strange.
I should have been more strange, I must confess,
But that thou overheard'st, ere I was ware,
My true-love passion. Therefore pardon me,
And not impute this yielding to light love,
Which the dark night hath so discovered.

Something in the room shifts as **Temi** *lets this performance go.*
Then she becomes highly camp once more.

Juliet. I dreamt of her every night.

Training with the Royal Youth Theatre
Was everything to me.
I was in their repertory company.
The premise of a rep
Is that one company
Does several plays
Giving the actors in the company
A chance to play many parts,
Of varying sizes,
To show off their range.
That year in every single show I was cast
. . . as a doctor.

Clinical. Practical. A person of few words.
Like my parents before me.

WHY! All the parts I ever got
At school, at university they were all BOYS.
RANDOM Functional MEN.
I am not a doctor.
I AM BLANCHE DUBOIS!
I am Juliet.

My heart is as boundless as the sea.
Why couldn't they see me?

But that didn't stop me.

I had the resilience, the grit and
The determination to keep going.
Plus I was told by multiple
Industry professionals that it was a –

She becomes an industry professional:

Temi   'Great time right now for . . .
(*Whispered.*) People of colour.'

Temi (*as herself*)   Right now.
A short window.
Limited time only.

I had to take advantage of it.

So I became a professional actress.

And this is the kind of part that I did play
When I started to work . . .

The lighting returns to a more intimate cabaret state.

Now for the next part of the show, I'm going to need a
member of the audience to come up on stage and join me to
read a few lines of dialogue. Would anyone be willing to do
that with me?

A member of the audience volunteers. **Temi** *gets the audience to
applaud them.*

Then she explains that they are going to be playing the part of the **Princess** *and offers them a crown to wear (optional).*

She explains that they are going to be reading Shakespeare but she emphasises that they shouldn't worry – everyone is looking at **Temi** *and no one is looking at them. She then explains that she's going to give them the text and the mic to speak into and they need to say their first line after* **Temi** *enters.*

The audience member plays the **Princess** *while* **Temi**, *in the hammiest way imaginable, plays* **Marcade**.

*

Princess
  Welcome, Marcade,
  But that thou interruptest our merriment.

Marcade
  I am sorry, madam, for the news I bring
  Is heavy in my tongue. The King your father—

Princess
  Dead, for my life.

Temi *(as* **Marcade***) looks furious that the audience member (the* **Princess***) has stolen her thunder.*

Marcade
  Even so. My tale is told.

*

Temi *ushers the audience member back to their seat, getting the audience to applaud them.*

Once the audience is settled, **Temi** *resumes.*

Temi   *That* was my *big* scene.

Love's Labour's Lost.

There are no small parts, only small actors.
Besides, I was no stranger to supporting roles.

I never did get the lead in the Year 6 leavers' play.
Millie did.

But I understudied the lead in *Love's Labour's*.
Killed.
The actress playing the lead was
Tragically killed.

I'm joking.
She just broke her leg.
Fell down the stairs on her way up to her dressing room.
WHOOPSIE!

But that meant . . .
I got to play her part
For an entire week!
It was amazing!
And I really saved that company's skin.
So I *knew* that the next time that company,
The Royal Shakespeare Company,
Was casting I'd be at the top of their list.

And the day came
When *Romeo and Juliet*
Was announced at The RSC.

I got to audition
For one of my favourite directors
ON MY BIRTHDAY.
15th of July, if you remember correctly.

It was star-crossed.
It was mine.
I could taste it.

When I left the audition room that day,
That hallowed day,
I knew I'd done everything I could do
To prepare.
I was a shoe-in.

She gets the microphone and her face drops.

Never
Heard
Back.

The lighting changes and she bursts into the chorus of 'Left Outside Alone' by Anastacia.

As the song ends with 'I need to pray', **Temi** *assumes a prayer position. Then lifts her head dramatically.*

*

Temi   ACT TWO: Losing my voice.

Blackout.

In the darkness, **Temi** *grabs the mic stand and puts the mic in its hold. As she taps the mic, the lights come up.*

A djembe underscore begins.

Temi   I come
From a community of people
That have been routinely
Silenced.
This one goes out to all my First Gs. *First . . .*
Generation
Babies.

Diaspora baby.
I'm a child
Of the di-ah-spora
Baby.

But I don't know how
To pronounce it.
Diaspora.
Di-ah-spora?
Diaspora dysphoria!
It's the most diaspora thing of all.
To not know –

*The **Stage Manager** starts clicking at **Temi** to get her attention. **Temi** notices but continues with her poem.*

Temi   How to say something right.
Something you live
Every day.
You can't say it right.
You can't do it right.
All these invisible rules.
Lasers
In the heist.
Duck dodge dive diaspora baby.
Di-ah-spora baybee.

*With masked concern, but inspired by the **Stage Manager**'s clicking:*

Temi   I love that clicking we've got going in the room.
Let's get everybody clicking.
Let's start a Mexican wave of clicks.
You start it here and send it around the space.
Lovely.

*The **Stage Manager** waves **Temi** over.*

Temi *heads over to them pretending everything is fine.*

She meets them at the side of the stage, all the while encouraging the audience to keep clicking.

*The **Stage Manager** whispers in **Temi**'s ear. The djembe underscore continues.*

Temi *returns to the stage, fake smile plastered on her face. She's buying time, trying to think, whilst doing unnecessary spins.*

She then decides to come clean to the audience.

Temi   I've just been told we're running slightly over. Because I was yammering on about masturbating at the top of the show. And we are fined £50 per minute that we run over. Is that right? I can't afford that!

So I'm just going to have to do some live cuts! I have to skip some bits.

Um . . . so yeah this poem, the rest of the poem is about being a child of the diaspora and a child of colonialism. How far my parents travelled to move here to give me a better life. The scarcity mentality. The Victorian parenting style. The Christian purity that they inherited from Step Mother Britannia, the cultural chasm between me and them.

Sorry. Han, can you cut the music please?

The **Stage Manager** *cuts the djembe underscore.*

Temi   This was the part of the show where I was going to flesh out their characters a bit more. My father, the author and star of my occasional bedtime stories. My mother's bombastic Yoruba fashions. The daily suppression of their selfhood. How they were just raising me the way they were raised. How no one probably ever asked them how they were feeling so how would they know to ask me.

Uh. Yeah I'll just do the last bit of the poem, Han . . .

She assumes a position onstage.

and then you call me & ask how i am
but I can't answer because
we never speak
in watercolour.

& then you ask me how's work
& when i'm going to buy a house.
sometimes it feels like
you're not looking in
on me but checking in
to see
whether your *huge* investment
is paying off.

Thank you.

OK, Han. If we just cut to the next spotlight cue, that would be great. Thanks.

*The **Stage Manager** cuts to a spotlight cue and **Temi** gets out a purple fluffy diary.*

Temi   Dear Diary,

Hello. Nice to meet you. My name is Temi and I am twelve years old.

You were a gift from my new best friend Poppy. I love your purple and fluff and big silver padlock. I love you and I promise to share all my thoughts and feelings and deepest darkest secrets with you. And one day, when I am dead and buried, someone will discover you and know who I was. And you'll be displayed in a museum and looked at by millions. You're going to be famous! But only if you keep my secrets. Love you bye.

*A brief instrumental underscore from Willow's 'Maybe It's My Fault' plays. As **Temi** assumes another position.*

Temi   Dear diary. I've got to confess. I think I masturbate. At church yesterday we heard about the sin of onan! He's the one in the Bible who spermed on the floor! but I don't have any sperm!

Poppy said what I've been doing is the same thing. Poppy always knows this kind of stuff. I couldn't ask Mum about it.

Gutted that I'm going to hell.

When I do don't sell my secrets to the tabloids.
Wait until the museums come, the curators of history.
Wait for them.

*A brief instrumental underscore from Willow's 'Maybe It's My Fault' plays. As **Temi** assumes another position.*

Dear Diary,

Last night was my first ever sleepover at Poppy's house. OMG. Her house is so nice! Her mum is so nice. Her dad is old.

We sat around the dinner table and ate together like a family from TV. Poppy's parents asked her all these questions about her day at school. Mum and Dad never ask me questions. They just care about how I do at school so they can brag about it to their friends. They're S-H-I-T.

A brief instrumental underscore from Willow's 'Maybe It's My Fault' plays. As **Temi** *assumes another position.*

Dear Diary,

I tried to talk to Poppy about Miss Henley. Last week she only gave me a detention for talking when me and Poppy were both talking. Poppy said Miss Henley just happened to look up when I was talking and I was just unlucky.

But today I got told off by Mrs Whistable for laughing too loud! On a theatre trip! She said I was so loud an elderly couple in front of me kept turning around to look.

She said I should use my inside laughing voice next time. I said OK.

A brief instrumental underscore from Willow's 'Maybe It's My Fault' plays. As **Temi** *assumes another position.*

Dear diary, all the teachers tell me off for no reason! It's like they just snap! Mrs Pearlman was like red in the face today. She looked like a dragon! Even Poppy noticed it this time!

But that's what always happens. With Mrs Pearlman, Miss Henley, Mr Bacon, Mrs Cartright, Mr Pasty, Miss Bland, Mrs Cracker, Mr Gammon . . . Almost all of my teachers! I don't get why.

I am always on my best behaviour, always smiley and polite, I always hand in my homework on time. It's like no one notices me trying. Sometimes it feels like there's something wrong.

With me.

'Maybe It's My Fault' by Willow finally blasts, with lyrics. As **Temi** *is launched into a contemporary dance/mime sequence:*

She tries to head to the microphone. But her body drags her away. She pulls a white mask from her trunk, despite herself. She puts the mask on her face. She is fighting it but the mask is strong.

She tries to get to the microphone but the mask is pulling her in a different direction. She wrestles it and tears it off. She runs and grabs the mic.

– Mum read my diary!
She broke the lock, ripped it open and read it.

Something shifts in her.

Why would she do that?

Nothing is safe. Nothing is sacred anymore.

A pause.

The Stage Manager   Temi. I'm sorry, we really need to move on –

Temi   No I will not move on! She barely ever spoke to me. Never *asked* me how I was feeling then she breaks into my diary and reads my innermost thoughts. Screamed at me for getting a detention! For touching myself! For calling her shit! Disrespecting her in the privacy of the padlocked diary she'd broken into! I never wrote in my diary again. How many great artists started off by writing in a diary? How many years of self-expression did she rob me of? Maybe I never got cast as anything other than one-dimensional supporting characters because I was a one-dimensional character. Functional. Serving everyone else's needs. Perfect for my parents so they would give me *any* attention, perfect for my teachers so they wouldn't punish me for no fucking reason! And the one place I *could* express my emotions, was onstage. But I never got the kind of parts where I could channel them because –

I was probably a bad actor! I was wearing a mask every single day without knowing it. I probably didn't know how to take it off and be vulnerable onstage. Or even if I could, no one would ever notice because I was always appealing to white institutions –

She catches herself. She looks into the audience stunned at her own temerity.

I didn't mean to say all of that. I am not an angry black woman, I'm not even an angry person! I am *so* grateful for this space. So grateful to my mum. I would not be standing here without her.

Soho Upstairs. Love you. Love you so much.

Oh my God. I've lost you. I've lost the entire audience.

She runs to the microphone.

This show is not about race. Or *oppression*.
It's about me!
It's about how deserving I am of attention . . .

(*Whispered.*) Fuck. You hate this.
You hate me.

(*With resolve.*) I'm going to get you back.
Um . . . uh . . .

She looks at the **Stage Manager**. *Then the audience.*

Temi   I'm going to do a dance.
Han! Cue the song at the end of the QLab.
It would have been the one for the fifth encore.

Don't worry, I'm going to finish on time!

The **Stage Manager** *plays 'Get Right' by Jennifer Lopez.* **Temi** *does an absurd dance routine.*

At a certain point, through hand gesture, **Temi** *gets the* **Stage Manager** *to cut the music.*

These next few sections of text can be largely improvised depending on the temperament of who you pick on.

Temi   Excuse me? Do you not like what I'm doing up here? It's just . . . you looked down. Yeah you did. It was just for a moment. But in that brief moment you were not looking at me. So . . .

That's OK. It happens. Just don't let it happen again. Thank you.

Temi *cues the* **Stage Manager** *to play the music again. She resumes her dance routine.*

Another audience member pisses her off. Through gesture, **Temi** *cuts the music through the* **Stage Manager**.

Temi   Something interesting over there? Did you come here to look at the set design. News flash! There isn't much of it, we are in the round! Could you – *focus on me. Baby, could you –* Is that OK? Thank you.

She cues the **Stage Manager** *to play the music again. This time she gets an idea.*

Rather than returning to her routine, through improvised dance, she shares various parts of her body, up close and personal, to receive the validation she craves.

This culminates in her thrusting her pubis at a white audience member. She stops.

Looks exasperated.

She signals for the **Stage Manager** *to cut the music.*

In silence, she gets up and grabs the microphone. She stares down the offending audience member.

Temi   You blinked.
You blinked and that . . .
Was racist.
Do you understand what it means for you,
As a white person*,

To close your eyes,
To shut off your consciousness
From witnessing my labour
As a black woman*.
That is fucked.

[*If performed on a Black Out Night (!) pick a man and just lose
the clause 'as a white person'.]

[Change the weaponised identity marker where necessary or just
comedically desired. e.g. as a black queer man, as a black trans
woman, etc.]

I'm going to need all of you
To look at me,
Really look at me
And not blink.

She stares one audience member down. They inevitably blink.

Temi howls like an animal in pain. She falls to the floor in agony
and crawls to a soft space onstage.

Why? Why would you do that? Are you trying to kill me?

She then speaks very softly into the microphone.

Maybe I need attention a bit too much. Cos I wasn't given
much as a child. Which they say is normal for performers.
But I think, for me, it's because of colonialism? But maybe
I'm wrong and it's got nothing to do with how the system
forces minorities to become . . . well, minorities. Machines.
Keeps them in survival mode, which forces them to repress
their emotions. Which, in turn, makes them repress the
emotions of their children. Which is what made *me* turn to
the stage. But the society that made me this way barred me
from the attention I so desperately crave because of all the
subtle, *silent* white supremacy within our institutions.

Or maybe I'm chatting shit and I'm just an attention whore!

She sighs.

I don't like talking about this stuff.
I wanted to talk about love.
I wanted to be Juliet.

I think I can get up.
I just need a bit of encouragement . . .

The audience cheer and encourage her.

You don't have to give me a standing ovation
But it would definitely help.

The audience clap and cheer louder; hopefully they give **Temi** *a standing ovation. If they do,* **Temi** *thanks them and tells them to 'Please be seated'.*

She takes a few sips of water and then, upon catching eyes with the **Stage Manager***, says:*

Temi   Oh my God, Han! I've completely derailed the show.
Again!
How much time have we lost?
Don't answer that.

We *have* to do Act Three. It's the denouement!

She turns to an audience member.

Do I need to fix my make-up?

(*Ad-lib depending on their reaction but ultimately* . . .)
You're lying! I feel so sweaty.

Han, if you could keep this same lighting state so I fix my face, I'm going to start Act Three and cue you when I want the lights to change.

I'll be super-quick, Act Three will be *light of foot.*

She gives an audience member a mirror to hold for her.

Can you hold this for me please? Thank you.

She dabs her face with a tissue.

This Final Act is entitled 'Embracing my body'.

I wasn't booking jobs.
Wasn't even getting auditions.
So I did what every self-respecting washout does
When they're down and out.
I hit the clubs.

The underscore of Craig David's 'Rewind' plays.

Temi   That's where I found myself.
Found my body.
My audience.
The dance floor is incredibly democratic.
But if you saw me
Moving out there
You'd never imagine
My rhythmic past.

We hear the eponymous lyrics: Re-ee-wind.

When the crowd say?

If the audience say: 'Bo' Selecta!' **Temi** *encourages them. Then she abruptly changes affect for sympathy.*

Temi   When I was a child
I was told I couldn't dance.
My parents would laugh
At me at the family functions.
They'd call me
Oyinbo,
Oreo,
Coconut.
It was humiliating!
Especially because it was
Their fault I was like that.
It's like when they'd laugh at me
For not being able to speak
Our language.
That's not on me, bitch!
That's on you!

She starts to make her way back to centre stage.

And, obviously,
Being told you can't dance makes you worse
At dancing because you become self-conscious about it.

She cues the **Stage Manager** *and 'Lose My Breath' by Destiny's Child begins to play quietly.*

Temi   I made it my life's mission
To become a great dancer.
I studied all the music videos
Every day after school on MTV Bass.
I tried to learn the Harlem Shake.

She attempts a terrible version of this.

The Dougie.

She attempts a terrible version of this.

The Dutty Wine.

This is the most absurd of all.

Music videos didn't teach me how to dance.
They taught me something better.
Main. Character. Energy.
That's right. It's happened.
The title of the show.

If you live your life
Like you're in a music video
– You're a star.
Whether you're listening to music on the train
Or in the middle of a packed dance floor.
If you move through the world like
Everyone is either
Obsessed with
Or in love with you,
You have Main Character Energy.

Maybe I wasn't bad at dancing.
Maybe I was just a child
Who was awkward in her body.
I just needed some confidence.

My mother would have killed
For my pubescent body.
She told me so all the time.

Her and my aunties would sit around
The kitchen counter
Counting each other's calories.
Comparing diet regimes.

I'd look at their full bellies,
Their thick thighs.
I didn't look like that.
I thought I had swerved my genetics.
I never thought . . . it would catch up with me!

'Tomboy' by Princess Nokia plays – 'My little titties and my fat belly'. **Temi**, *in awed horror and against her own will, is pulled up by her chest and stomach.*

No one warns you how your body changes
When you age.
I was aging out of the ingenue
And one day I woke up
With a body like my aunties.

But I'm a bad bitch
And so are you. I'm a bad bitch. And I'm built
Like Winnie the Pooh.

'Tomboy' by Princess Nokia plays again.

Temi, *initially against her own will, dances along. Then comes to enjoy her titties and belly in the movement.*

So in the prime of my life
And the pit of my career
I started dancing.

Every week you'd find me in the club.
Queer dance floors.
Throwing my ass back.
I had no fucks left to give.

That's where I realised
There's no such thing as a bad dancer.
Some of you aren't hearing me.
In these rooms we're accepting of all rhythms, of all bodies,
The perfection of a person lies
In the particularity of their imperfections.
And so it is
In our dance.

If you've caught the spirit
You've caught the spirit.
If you're lost in the moment.
We can see it.
We can share it.
Even if you're a little offbeat.

That's cute.
If it's true to you.
True to the moment.

That's where I started feeling sexy.
Enjoying my body.
Enjoying being in it.

I started feeling more femme.
All those boy parts at school, at university,
Had changed the way I carried myself.
I grew my hair out.
Adorned myself.

But I'd still look out
For Juliet.
Every time it was programmed
I'd email the director.
Three months before first preview.

Sometimes I'd get seen.
I'd watch other people get cast.
Sometimes they were black.
Light skinned.
I'd be so jealous.
Then it happened . . .
A dark-skinned Juliet.
The pride I felt
And the envy.
But fuck.

This is what happens
When you're more than functional.
When you're not just there to serve the story.
When you are the story.
The Main Character.
They tell you how they see you.

The torrents of abuse.
Pages of it.
Scrolling and scrolling.
My thumb hurt.
And I still fucking want it!

She has stunned herself. She wasn't supposed to say this.

Stage Manager   Temi.

Temi *looks at the* **Stage Manager**. *A breath.*

Temi   Fuck it. Give me a spot.

She gestures to the **Stage Manager** *to give her a spotlight. She sits in the reflective light.*

I still want it.
Despite the racism.
Despite the hell.
Waking up to death threats.
Comments about your nose,
Your body,

Your blackness,
Your womanhood.

I still want Juliet so much
That I would take the abuse.
Willingly.
What does that say about me?
Maybe this is what happens
When your parents sell your soul.
When they send you to private school
Cos they think it's the
Best way for their black child
To exceed in a system that
Works against them.
You become so othered,
So desperate for validation
That you would do *anything* to be seen.
To achieve.
Maybe even turn on your own.

Am I just a *camp Kemi Badenoch*?

She grabs the blanket at her feet and comforts herself with it.

Juliet won't make me safe.
She won't make me beautiful.
She won't make me white.

She looks at the audience.

I love her because she's funny.
She's so funny.

She wants to shift the energy.

Can I have some more light please?

She begins to tie the blanket around her waist.

I don't need an ending.
That would be too convenient.
The powers that be would love that!
No.

This is post-modern.

She stands up to reveal that the blanket has transformed into a gorgeous skirt.

And I've done it.
I've made my own show.
Ad-libs and all.
I am *healed*!

I've got you to look at me.

She looks at the audience.

But I don't know how you're looking at me.
I don't know
If you see me as
A clown or
A clown.

She exhales.

She's done with this.

She's done with not being truly seen.

She starts to take off her skirt and resolves to leave the stage.

But as she sets the skirt down on the chest, something about it feels reminiscent of dress-up, of the make-believe.

This simple action has transformed this piece of furniture to something new. Something beautiful.

She takes in a breath.

I'm just going to pretend.
I'm going to pretend
You see me the way I see me.
In all my playfulness.
In all my boundlessness.
In all my beauty.

You see me that way. Because,
Yeah.

I've decided.
You are
An audience of mes.

She takes the audience in, makes a decision and lies down on the chest. She starts to masturbate. She moans indulgently.

This mounts into a scream:

I'm amazing. I'm amazing!

Stage Manager   Temi . . . we're officially out of time.

Temi *continues masturbating indulgently.*

Temi   I'm amaziiiiiing!

She orgasms.

'Float' by Janelle Monáe begins to play as **Temi** *melts onto the floor.*

She rises into an iconic, sexual and expansive movement sequence that culminates in her dancing powerfully for herself in a shower of bubbles.

As she jumps gleefully into the air, we blackout.

Fin.

Playwright's Acknowledgements

Firstly to Dom Martin, for taking the picture of me that set this journey into motion. Seeing myself captured like that in my joy and in my power – it has low-key changed my life. Thank you!

Thank you to Katie Sinclair for telling me, over the phone, that that picture was giving 'Main Character Energy'. You've probably forgotten it but you definitely inspired the title, which came well before the show.

Thank you to Jo Nastari for sitting and dreaming with me at Hawkwood when the seeds of this began.

Thank you to Travis Alabanza for *so much*. But particularly for introducing me to Bobby Harding, the Angel of my Dreams.

Thank you, Bobby Harding, for being the most caring, creative and powerful producing witch, vocal coach and loving friend on this epic journey. I love you, diva!

Thank you, Ragevan Vaikunthavasan. My old friend, platonic boyfriend and the most precise, intuitive and hilarious director (and dramaturg) I have ever worked with. There is no one I would rather have done this daring dance with than you.

Thank you to those who inspired me in the development of this show: Kate Berlant, John Early, Durand Bernarr, RAYE, Charli XCX, Beyoncé and bell hooks to name but a few.

Thank you to Dimple Pau for giving me the space to share and start this journey. To early dramaturgs Celine Lowenthal, Nina Bowers, Katie Greenall and Jane Fallowfield. My early encouragers Tom Rasmussen, Miriam Battye, Theo Schofield, Jack Parlett, Vanessa Kissule and Sophie Duker.

To Charlotte, Katie, Ellie Manwah and everyone at Paines Plough, the whole team in and around the Roundabout of Summer '24.

To Lee Griffiths and everyone you brought into Soho for labs, but particularly Elf Lyons. Thank you, both, for daring me to dream this into its most gleaming being.

Everyone at Soho! From the bar staff, to the marketing and producing teams to the front of house.

To Lily, Caoimhe and Mark.

Bambi, Jasmine, Lauren, Xana – my avengers! Thank you. You truly assembled.

And Annika, Amani and Kam who joined the team for Soho. You all ate and left no crumbs.

To Travis, again, for hosting the Black Out Night. A dream come true. I can't wait to do it again in Bristol and to do so many, many more times.

Wabriya, thank you for helping me make this show both safe and silly. Natasha, and all the other therapists I've worked with, thank you so much for helping me love myself and, in turn, truly love others.

Thank you to my mother and father who worked so hard so I could get whatever I dreamed and loved me the way they knew how.

Thank you to my sister, Toni, who is perfect.

And finally, to quote Snoop Dogg, I want to thank me.

I want to thank me for believing in me, for working so hard and for loving on myself, despite it all. <3